Hazard Ahead

Written and photographed by Andy Hall

Hazard Ahead

Published in 2008 by A. Hall Publishing, Crowborough, East Sussex

Design and production by JAC Design, Clockhouse Court, Beacon Road, Crowborough, East Sussex, TN6 1AF   www.jacdesign.co.uk

ISBN 978-0-9558474-0-0

Hazard Ahead

CONTENTS

Hazard Ahead

INTRODUCTION TO LEARNING TO UNDERSTAND THE ROADS

Welcome to the Hazard Ahead Book, which I hope you will find a useful add-on tool to your other driving aids.

THERE'S A LOT TO LEARN

To learn to drive you must have a Provisional Driving Licence. If you have never been at the controls of a car before you will find that there is a lot to absorb in the first 10 or so hours of lessons. The ability to coordinate your eyes, hands and feet all at the same time is rather like playing a complex piece of music on a cathedral organ! Concentration is at a high level right from when you move away from the kerb for the first time.

To use the steering wheel correctly and at the same time be able to check what is going on behind you with your mirrors as well as changing gear is a mental stress reaction that can be hard to overcome in the early stages of driving a vehicle. Moreover, remembering the correct sequence of doing the things required as a driver can be a marathon task. No one would expect the memory system of the human brain to take in all the instructions given the instant you start to drive. To enter a busy road with different types of junctions is mind boggling to say the least!

If you are using a private car, you must be accompanied by a driver with a Full Licence and a minimum of three years experience following the date he/she passed the practical test. The car must have 'L' Plates attached front and back. Remember you are not allowed on motorways with a provisional licence.

THE RIGHT FRAME OF MIND

Having the right frame of mind is very important. You need to have a calm approach to dealing with the pressures that build up inside you while travelling on the roads. Keeping your cool is the key to your survival. Never assume you have "right of way" over anyone. Avoid "road ownership". Everyone has a right to be on the roads. Having the right attitude is not a weakness, but a feeling of strength by being in command of yourself and aware of what is going on around you.

The ability to scan ahead as well as seeing what is going on behind you while driving is all part of your skills as a safe and competent driver. Secondly, to identify a risk, then plan how to deal with it methodically, should be part of your decision-making. Without the ability to plan in good time and totally concentrate on dealing with a particular risk means that you are moving into an "accident zone". Never assume that all drivers are going to behave in the manner you might expect. You might feel annoyed or frustrated by their actions, but you just have to avoid challenging them or competing. A car might overtake you even though you are travelling up to the speed limit of the road. Overtaking is a dangerous and, in many ways, an unnecessary manoeuvre, but in this situation never increase your speed to prevent them from doing this.

DEFENSIVE DRIVING

Defensive driving is the best way to be safe. Even if you have priority over oncoming traffic you might have to slow down or even stop if necessary to avoid confrontation.

PROGRESSIVE DRIVING

Driving too slowly is not good practice and will entice good drivers to overtake you unnecessarily. Keeping up with the traffic flow will help drivers behind you do the same and reduce the risk of an accident. If you can do 40 mph in a 40 mph speed limit then do it! Why go slower?

Progressive driving is what the police like and so, of course, do the examiners! Clearing a junction in a positive way is good driving.

PLANNING AHEAD

Planning a drive is essential especially if you are taking unfamiliar roads. Having up-to-date maps will help you prepare the journey sensibly. Allow plenty of time to study the best routes. A long trip should be prepared at least the day before you depart. Then allow almost more time than needed to make the trip. Leaving the journey late will create a dangerous drive. Your thoughts on road safety will be over-ridden by anxieties and frustration. You could experience traffic delays that could seriously hamper your arrival time.

STATE OF HEALTH

It is vitally important that you are in good health, in sound mind and not suffering from depression, fatigue or stress. If, for example, you have suffered as a result of losing a friend or a member of the family then you will quite likely find driving difficult to do well, because your mind will not be fully in focus with the roads. There are other issues that could have a detrimental effect on your concentration to drive like financial worries, examination results, peer groups and work uncertainties.

LOOKING AFTER YOUR CAR

Car maintenance is also a very important aspect behind your ability to drive. Never drive with a very low fuel level. Remember, you may find yourself delayed in getting to a garage due to unforeseen problems on the roads. Make sure you understand the minimum legal treads of tyres. Any shredding around the tyres means you must get them replaced. You must know what the minimum oil level is and where to look for it. The windscreen washer fluid must be topped up from time to time as well as the coolant. The contents of these reservoirs must contain antifreeze. The horn and lights must be in working order. It is quite common to have a brake light out, because they tend to heat up when used a lot. Ask someone to check if the brake lights are working as you apply the foot brake.

Remember your car must be taxed and currently insured before you can drive on the public roads.

HAZARD PERCEPTION

Hazard Perception covers all aspects of driving. You should be able to observe and identify a potential risk in good time, scanning the road as far as you can see, not just in front of the car. A bend in the road or a bright sun streaming through the windscreen in between shadows are both hazards.

In this book I have gathered many different hazard situations which you should take into account and know how to deal with. It's a matter of "reading the road".

You may use the same road every day of the year, but there will be a time when you might encounter something right out of the blue. Be prepared for any possible changes. Road works, a fallen tree, or flooding are grouped as temporary hazards. Speed limits, road markings and road narrowing are categorised as more permanent hazards. It is very easy to look ahead but not so easy to look to the side of the road.

Missing an important sign could make your drive difficult and even dangerous. In the summer months a speed sign could be covered by the growth of a hedge. Temporary road signs may be in place to alert drivers of road works ahead. Expect to stop due to a temporary traffic light sign before a bend.

Hazard Perception is now part of the Driving Theory Test so you will need to prepare for it in your own time. You cannot take the Practical Test until you have passed the Theory Test.

QUESTIONS

At the end of the book there are questions grouped under various headings that you will find throughout the following pages. A few questions may require you to search for the information outside this book, although you may find them straightforward and easy to understand.

I would strongly suggest that you go through the subjects for each group of questions in stages. If you are learning to drive with a school, then go through a set of questions either before or after completing the practical on a particular subject. You will benefit by running both practical and theory side by side. If your instructor tells you that the next lesson will be on Crossroads, you could go through the section on Crossroads and then answer the questions before putting it into practice.

In the case of dealing with Roundabouts go to "http://www.roundabouts-tutorial.com" and have a look at the various interactive tutorials.

Use of Indicators

1 At all junctions you must indicate if it is Major – Minor, or Minor – Major. Make sure you indicate correctly and it must be well timed after you have checked your mirrors.

2 You must indicate correctly. If you are taking the second road to the left, then indicate as you pass the first road. If you indicate too early then cars might pull out from the first road thinking you are going to enter their road.

3 If you are going to turn right at the end of the road, then indicate as you are passing the road on your right. If you indicate too early then vehicles could pull out from that road before you pass. Also a vehicle beside the kerb in your road some way ahead of you could pull out thinking you are going into the minor road.

1 In a general drive you should check behind with your mirrors every six to eight seconds. It need only be a "one" second glance. The main (interior) mirror is a flat glass. What you see here is a true size image as if you had turned your head and looked between the two front seats. You need to check your mirrors before you apply brake pressure or increase your speed. Also a mirror check is important before you change your position in the road. You have to be aware of any vehicle that might look as if it wants to overtake you. A car that is close behind you should be a concern to you, especially if you have to slow down.

2 The wing mirrors are convex, which means vehicles will look as if they are further away from you than they really are. The left and right wing mirrors cover some areas that you can also see in your main mirror, but also along the side of the car. The further back you see in all your mirrors the zone of vision widens. But there are areas to the sides of your car that are not covered at all by any of the mirrors. We call these blind spots. This is why it is crucial to physically turn your head and look over your left shoulder and over your right shoulder, before moving away from a parking position. You will also need to do shoulder looks when changing lanes in one-way streets or along dual carriageways and motorways.

3 Here you can see a van going into a blind spot on your right.

4 A car passing on your right is in a blind spot.

5 This car is going into a blind spot.

6 On approaching an obstruction on your side of the road look briefly into your main and right mirrors before positioning out to go around the obstruction. You are looking for a vehicle like a motorbike, which might intend to overtake you. Use your main and left mirrors for coming back in. You need to check for anything like a cyclist or a pedestrian, whom you might not have seen on the initial approach. Just as important is to make sure you have cleared the vehicle.

7 If you are taking a road to the left, check your main and left mirrors, as you also would for pulling up against a kerb.

8 Keep a frequent "eye" on what is going on behind you.

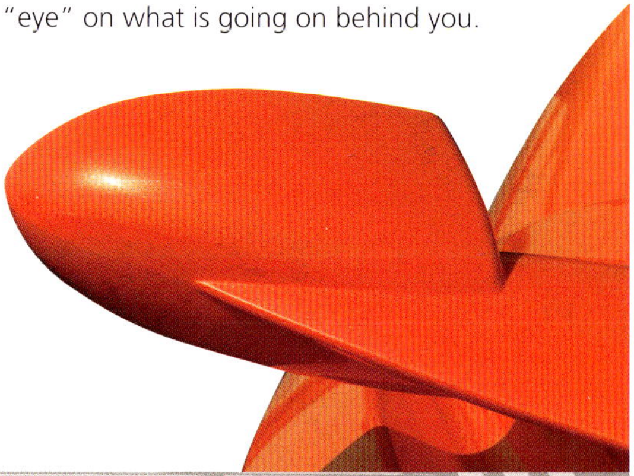

9 Now you see a motorbike coming up behind you. Anticipate it is going to overtake you. A bike in this position could be seen in both your main and right mirrors.

10 There are three very important actions you must avoid whilst being overtaken: 1) Do not increase your speed; 2) Do not apply a right indicator; 3) Do not steer the car towards the centre of the road. Allow the motorcyclist to pass you.

11 The car behind you is only a few feet away.

12 Know what is going on behind you at all times.

1 Unmarked T Junction – Take early effective observation. This junction is found in quiet and rural areas. You need to act defensively and prepare to stop at the junction even though no one has priority.

2 The Give Way Sign – There is no compulsory requirement for you to stop but taking good observation will allow you to decide whether to stop or move into the major road with caution.

3 The Stop Sign – This sign signifies a mandatory stop must be made at the T Junction. This is probably due to a restricted view either to the right or left at the point of entry into the major road. It does not mean that the major road is any busier.

4 The Stop Sign on the road surface. Note the thick white line across the lane. The requirement is to stop at this line.

5 A Controlled T Junction – This junction is controlled by traffic lights due to high volume of traffic. Note the Yellow Box (see Yellow Box Chapter) and the No Right Turn Sign.

6 Approaching a Give Way Junction to turn right. Note that the car is positioned just to the left of the lines in the centre of the road. The Give Way markings comprise an inverted triangle and broken lines at the point of entry. Look right – left – right and do this as many times as necessary before making a decision to enter the major road.

7 Another Controlled T Junction.

8 Approaching the T junction to turn left. Note the position of the car is close to the kerb. You should follow the kerb at the corner so that at the point of entry the car is positioned with a slight left steer.

Junctions Minor to Major

9 Looking along the thick white line at a compulsory stop T junction.

10 Looking right at the stop T junction.

11 This is a view looking towards the point of entry at the stop junction. Note the speed limit in the major road is 40 mph. The minor road in this picture is restricted to 30 mph.

12 The broken lines and inverted triangle at the point of entry means you must give way to traffic in the major road.

13 Looking left at the stop junction. Note that a car is coming. You must allow this car to pass. Note also the pedestrian crossing on the left. Possibly the reason for this junction being a mandatory stop one is to draw your attention to the close proximity of the crossing, especially for turning left.

14 Allow the estate car to enter your road. That car has priority over you as it is on the major road.

15 Position the car at the junction where the bottom part of the black frame of the mirror appears to look as if it is over the white lines.

16 Looking to your right you see an uncontrolled pedestrian crossing. When turning right, drive cautiously taking good observation around the crossing.

1 Turning left from the major road into the minor road. At the corner look for pedestrians and give way to them crossing at the junction. Steer the car slowly and look down the left side lane of the minor road. Use brisk steering. Remember wherever you look will draw the car in that direction. So avoid looking down the middle of the minor road.

2 Turning right from the major road into the minor road. Make sure the front of the car is in line with the centre of the minor road before steering right and looking along the left lane.

3 Concentrate looking down the left lane as you steer and look for any obstructions such as parked vehicles.

4 Notice this car has cut the corner by turning too early.

5 You are going to take the next road to your right, but you see a car coming in the opposite direction on the major road. Assess the speed and distance of the approaching car and prepare to stop your car before turning into the minor road. Oncoming traffic has priority over you.

6 Enter the middle lane to turn right and give way to the oncoming car.

Pedestrian Crossings

1 This is a Zebra Crossing. You can identify this crossing by the yellow 'blinking' beacons on poles either side of the crossing. Also the actual crossing has black and white markings on the road surface. This crossing is uncontrolled; in other words it has no traffic lights. The only control at these crossings is carried out by the pedestrian. If a pedestrian has one foot on the crossing treat it like a red light and approach to stop. Here you can see this crossing is set very close to a junction to the left. This is a place where pedestrians tend to cross the road in reasonable numbers. These crossings can be positioned almost anywhere in a built up area and are found in 30 mph speed limit zones.

2 This is a Zebra Crossing with an island in the middle. Treat this crossing as a double crossing. In other words each half is a separate crossing. Approach at a speed you could stop safely if a pedestrian is entering the island from your right. Approach to stop if you see a pedestrian waiting by the crossing on your left.

3 This is a Staggered Zebra Crossing. This should be treated as two crossings. The island is long enough for pedestrians to move along to the next crossing position.

4 This is a Controlled Staggered Crossing. Again treat this as two separate crossings. You can see it is controlled by traffic lights that can be activated by the pedestrian pushing a button. It can be either a Puffin or Pelican type. A Pelican has a flashing amber light that follows a red light. That means anyone on the crossing must be allowed to continue walking to the other side. The lights controlling one side of the road are independent of the other lights.

5 This is a Controlled Pelican Crossing, the oldest of the controlled crossings. As you approach this crossing look to the right side and you will see a yellow box. If a pedestrian presses the button you will see the "wait" sign light up. If the sign is on then you can expect the lights will change to amber, then red at any time. Be aware someone could have pressed the button but sees the road is clear and as a result crosses the road before the lights have changed. Even if there is no one there you must stop at the crossing if the lights change to red.

6 You are approaching another Pelican Crossing. Check your mirrors before slowing down. Look for pedestrians close to the crossing. You can see a person on your left just to the right of the light. Even if you are not able to see the wait sign approach at a speed you could stop safely if necessary.

7 "See a Red Light – Show a Red Light". This is a good catch-phrase. In other words wherever you see a red light, whether it is from the brake lights of a car or a traffic light, you apply braking in response. You can see the lights of a Pelican Crossing have turned red. Approach at a speed you can stop just before the painted white line you can see across your lane of the road. The Pelican Crossing is timed when lights are red. From red the lights will move to flashing amber for a few seconds. Allow anyone on the crossing to continue to the other side. Be very observant as you might see a pedestrian start to cross at this point from the pavement. This is not correct from the pedestrian point of view but you need to anticipate this could happen before you start to move. You must not park or overtake within the Zig-Zag Lines.

8 After passing the crossing make sure it is safe to overtake if necessary.

9 You need to be aware that some crossings are positioned close to the doors of shops or banks. This is a Zebra Crossing close to a bank door. You need to approach this crossing at "walking pace" (less than 10 mph). Scan the sides of the road for people. Approach at a speed where you can stop safely if necessary.

10 This is a view looking down towards a Zebra Crossing. On the right side is a pedestrian area with a restricted view due to the buildings. Anticipate that a person could arrive at a moment's notice, so you should be driving at walking pace and making constant observations to your right and left.

11 Prepare to stop at the white line.

12 This is a Toucan Crossing. This crossing takes pedestrians as well as cyclists.

13

14

15

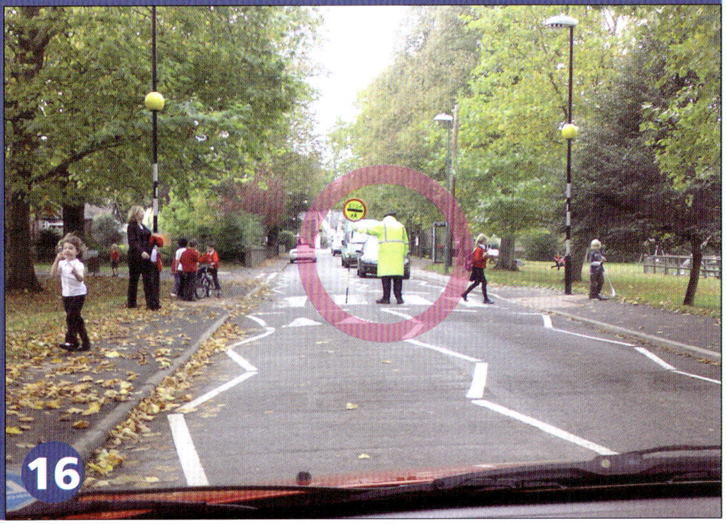
16

13 Approach this crossing very slowly. Notice that a lorry has stopped and blocked your view to the right. Lean forward in your seat and look to the right as you arrive at the crossing. Anticipate someone could appear any second.

14 As you can see there is a Zebra Crossing which is positioned close to a mini roundabout. Coming from the roundabout you need to be very focused on the crossing. Approach at a speed where you could stop safely if necessary.

15 Stop within the distance you see to be clear: "Tyres and Tarmac". See the back wheels and some road of the car in front. The emphasis on clearance has been set out in the Adequate Clearance Section. But at a pedestrian crossing the scenario is if you are "rear end shunted" by a vehicle behind you, you could be pushed on to the crossing causing injury to a person on the crossing.

16 At a children patrol you could expect a Lollipop Man or Lady. They are dressed in bright yellow so that they can be clearly seen. You could expect to see them as children are heading off for school in the morning between 8.30 am and 9 am. In the afternoon you could see them around 3 pm and 3.30pm. Remember when they come out into the road they carry the Law with them. It is a serious offence if you ignore their request for cars to stop.

The Yellow Box

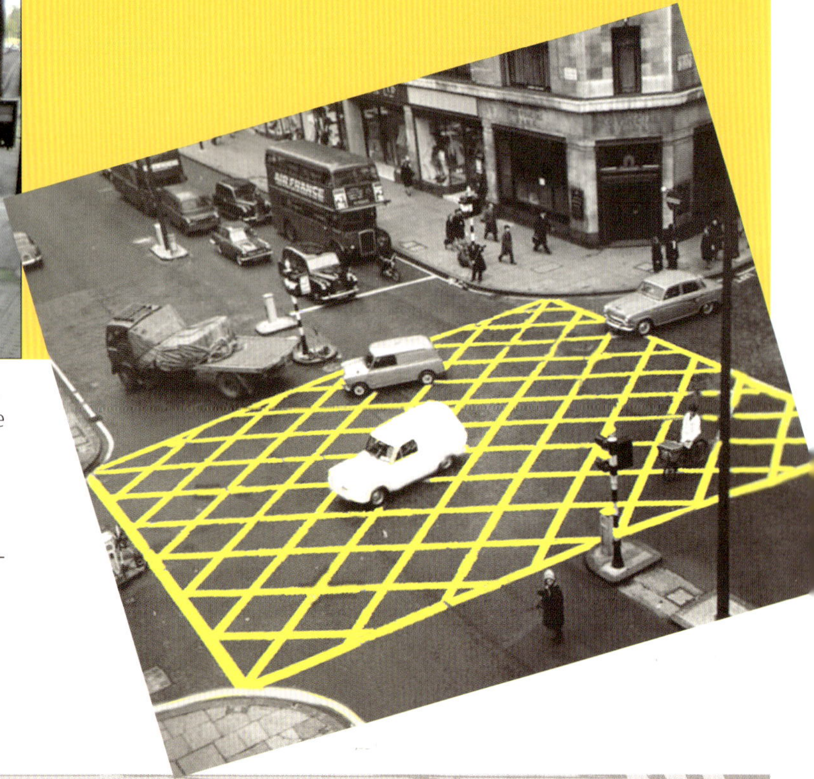

1 The Yellow Box means you cannot enter the box unless your exit is clear, even if the traffic lights on your side go to green. In this picture you need to have a look down the road to your right and check for any possible traffic congestion building up. It looks clear here so you can proceed.

2 The only time you can stop in the Yellow Box is when you are turning right from the major road into the minor road.

3 This is a Yellow Box controlled crossroad.

The Horn

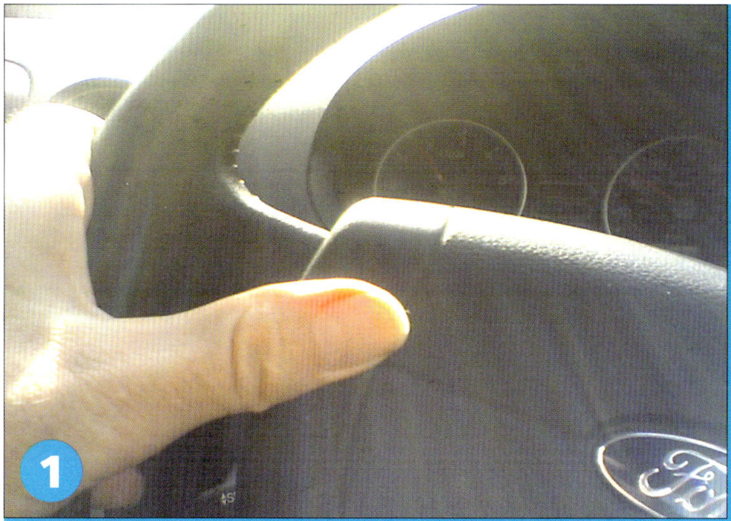

1 Use the horn to warn people of your presence. The horn should not be used in anger or frustration. Use it in the event of a potentially dangerous situation occurring. For example, a car reversing out into your road, where you feel the driver has not seen you. A good place you could use the horn in moderation is along a narrow road with high hedges and sharp bends. A short blip on the horn before a sharp bend will warn people on the road ahead to pull into the side or alert a car coming in the opposite direction. The horn must not be used between 11.30 pm and 7 am.

Crossroads

1 A crossroad sign - The thick vertical line states that you are on the major road. The thin horizontal line represents the two minor roads.

2 Here you have a partially unmarked crossroad – Look for gaps in the hedges to identify the road running from left to right while on the approach. Take good observation on the approach and prepare to give way if necessary.

3 You are approaching a "give way" crossroad. The major road runs from left to right. Neither you nor a car in the opposite minor road has any priority over one another. It is really a case of who moves first. Have eye contact with a driver opposite and see if the car opposite starts to move first. Hold position if a car opposite turns to its right which will cross in front of you. At the junction look first to your right then left, ahead and right again. Do this, as many times as necessary before deciding whether it is safe to enter. This observation procedure will apply whether you are going right, left or ahead.

4 A Stop Sign. This means you must completely stop the car once you have arrived at the point of entry and then carry out your observation. The purpose of a mandatory stop requirement is to draw your attention to a restricted view. It does not mean that the major road is busy. There could be a blind bend to your left or right.

5 A compulsory stop junction is marked by a thick white line across the left lane. Both the minor roads in this picture have stop markings because the vehicles from these roads are directly opposite one another.

6 Here is a controlled crossroad. Traffic lights are in place at all four entry points because the junction is too busy with traffic flow to have it in any other way. There is no major road as such.

7 Here you are approaching a staggered crossroad. This junction has the two minor roads not directly in line with each other.

8 Looking down the major road. The car on the left has to give way to the car on the major road.

9 In this picture you see that the two cars in the middle of the picture are turning right 'offside to offside'. That means they pass each other on the drivers' side. This procedure usually happens when the junction has opposing roads directly in line with one another. The only drawback with this procedure is that you cannot always see down the road you want to enter.

10 Turning right: 'nearside to nearside'. Arrows painted on the road surface pointing to the right and split by a diagonal line normally mark out this junction. This junction has roads to the left and right not directly opposite one another. Here the red car follows the direction of the arrow. The problem with this procedure is that there is limited view around the car opposite. You have to 'peep and creep'. Try and look through the car opposite and also look for reflections of vehicles coming round from behind.

11 Note the thick white lines at the point of entry signifying that you must stop due to the opposite minor road being offset. The opposite cars will directly face the cars at the point of entry in the bay on the right.

12 Looking down the major road. The two minor roads are to the left and right of the major road.

13 The junction has a mandatory stop sign on the approach, because there is a restricted view to the right.

14 This is a controlled crossroad with a yellow box (see chapter on the Yellow Box). Only enter the box if your exit is clear otherwise hold back and do not enter even if the lights go green.

Country Roads

1 This is a ford. Drive through this area slowly in first or second gear and apply your foot brake several times, as soon as you are clear of the water, to check that it has not been weakened.

2 Damaged road surface means that heavy vehicles use this road.

3 Notice a man on the road with a dog. Remember country roads do not have pavements or paths for pedestrians to walk along. Notice also that there is a bend in the road ahead. Give good clearance around the walker and overtake when you have a good view down your road. Anticipate that the dog could break loose from its lead.

4 "More paint more danger". The lines on the side of the road are to alert you of potential hazards ahead like sharp bends with high hedges on either side, or approaching a junction. The brief use of the horn before you enter a sharp bend will alert pedestrains around the other side to pull over to the edge of the road or to tell an oncoming car of your presence.

5 Anticipate a vehicle around the bend.

6 You must maintain good clearance from the tractor. This will help you see around the vehicle.

7 Adequate clearance is important, because the tractor may pull over in a limited space (which might not be able to accommodate your car) to allow a vehicle to pass.

8 Keep a clearance of two to three car lengths back. That will allow you to see around the tractor. Notice a bend to the right ahead. You can also see a break in the hedge on the left.

9 Muddy surface on the road is possibly from agricultural vehicles. So anticipate tractors coming and going from the entrance on the left.

10 Mud on the road here could mean tractors or other off-road vehicles using the entrance on the right.

11 There is a bend to the left, but scan ahead to the distant hedge beyond the field. The hedge indicates where the road is going. Look for vehicles approaching from the opposite direction. This will give you time to pull over.

12 In the high growth of the summer or when the weather has been wet and windy anticipate fallen branches on the road.

13 Try to scan as far along the road as you are able to. Prepare to slow down in good time as you approach the bridge. NEVER ASSUME YOU HAVE RIGHT OF WAY. Many country roads have bridges that are too narrow to accommodate vehicles passing from opposite directions. Some bridges have a rise and dip road going across. The use of the horn briefly on the final approach could warn anyone ahead of your presence. Approach at a speed you could stop safely if necessary.

14 You are approaching another bridge. You should observe to see the road beyond is restricted, especially towards the right. Also the entrance is narrow. Start to reduce your speed and prepare to give way to a large vehicle coming in the opposite direction.

15 The road ahead has a restricted view and bends to the left. Always slow into a bend. Notice the shadows on the road, which could limit your ability to see pedestrians on the road.

16 Scan for speed signs and make sure you are at the speed before the sign if the speed for the road has been reduced. Here you should be at 40 mph about now. If however, you are in a lower speed limit before the 40 mph signs you must maintain the lower speed until you have passed the signs.

17 There is a sharp bend to the left so you should slow down in good time. If you enter a bend too fast, you could find yourself unable to negotiate the corner safely and possibly enter a skid. Try to look over the fence on the left to see where the road goes and look for oncoming traffic. Notice that the road surface looks wet on both sides.

18 Notice a sign on the right indicating a Public Footpath. Therefore anticipate walkers coming and going in this area. Also the road is shaded by growth on the right side so you could expect some ice on the road surface during the winter months.

19 While you are driving you should be scanning along each side of the road for signs. Remember signs that are triangular in shape are warning signs and ones with a circular shape are mandatory information like speed signs. The one that you see here covers two warnings that you must take into account. The top sign is warning you that pedestrians could be walking along the road. The lower sign beneath is warning you that your side of the road is narrowing. As you look a little further you will notice a sign with a red arrow pointing upwards and a black arrow pointing downwards. This means that oncoming traffic has priority over you. Observe that the road surface is muddy so expect vehicles coming and going from the right.

20 You are approaching a bridge. But there is also a dip in the road, which is called 'Dead Ground'. This restricts your view further along the road. Anticipate that a small vehicle like a motorbike could be coming up in the opposite direction in the middle of the road.

21 The long broken lines are to alert you of hazards ahead like sharp bends or junctions.

22 Ahead of you is a dip in the road (Dead Ground). But you can see the road further along in the distance.

23 You should notice the two signs ahead on the left. The first sign is informing you that both sides of the road are narrowing. The second sign is informing you that there is a double bend first to the right and then to the left.

24 As you maintain good scanning along the road you see sheep grazing to the right. It is very important to approach at a speed where you could stop safely if necessary. Keep the engine 'revs' low to avoid frightening the animals. Note the maximum speed for the road is 40 mph.

Country Roads

25 Double solid white lines in the middle of the road means no overtaking on your side and also for traffic coming in the opposite direction. You may only overtake small vehicles like cyclists, horses or milk floats travelling 10 mph or less but with caution.

26 Lines separating the lanes on both sides allow vehicles to position in the middle of the road to turn right.

27 Public footpath on the left, so look out for walkers on the road.

28 A sign warning drivers of a railway crossing ahead. The amber light comes on first followed by alternating red lights. The gates will start to drop.

29 Give good clearance to the gates.

30 The train at the crossing.

31 A Flood Warning sign. This could be a warning of a ford or a low-lying road bridge over a river or stream. Reduce your speed and scan the road ahead.

One-Way Streets

1 This is a One-Way Street. The clue is the sign of a white arrow with a blue background. The road you see here is very narrow and would not be suitable for two-way traffic. There are parked cars on either side that makes driving only possible in the middle of the road.

2 You must not enter this road. These are No Entry signs. The traffic flow will come in the opposite direction.

3 This is another No Entry sign.

4 The No Left Turn sign is warning you that the next road is a One-Way Street with traffic approaching in the opposite direction.

6 This is a One-Way Street with two lanes. Both lanes have straight arrows on the road surface. You need to plan in good time which lane you want to be in. If you want to move to the right lane, make sure you look into your main and right mirrors plus a right shoulder look to cover all the blind spots and indicate right if it is safe to do so. Then conduct the manoeuvre to the right lane.

1 This is a Warning Sign informing you that the road is narrowing from both sides of the road. Scan well down the road and reduce speed and never assume you have right of way. Approach at a speed where you could stop safely if necessary.

2 A mandatory sign stating you must give way to oncoming traffic.

3 Prepare to stop if you see a vehicle approaching in the opposite direction. Try to scan where the road is going. Here have a look over the black and white barrier in the direction of the church.

4 There are road works on the left around a bend. Approach at a speed where you could stop safely if necessary. Remember, with an obstruction on the left side of the road oncoming traffic has priority over you.

Meeting Traffic

5 When there are parked cars on both sides of the road no one has priority. But you must act defensively. Look for a space you could 'nudge' into on the left to allow a car to pass from the opposite direction. Alternatively, look for a space on the right side to hold back and allow a vehicle to enter from the opposite direction. Here you can see a space on the left that you can steer into. Position yourself slightly in and slightly out. Do not position yourself as if you are going to park as vehicles from behind might pass you, giving them the impression that you have finished your drive.

6 If there are cars already approaching you between parked cars, allow them to pass you.

7 Some bridges are narrow, but have no priority system. Have a good look along the road before entering the restricted area. Give way to a vehicle that has arrived there first. Notice the bend to the left ahead and a junction on the right. Cross the bridge slowly.

8 Again no one here has any priority between parked cars on both sides of the road. Prepare to stop before you arrive in the narrow area if you see a vehicle coming in the opposite direction. There is a gap on the left just beyond the first two cars. This is a space you could enter to give way to an oncoming vehicle. Flashing your head lights is not recommended, as it is confusing. It simply means "Warning. I am here".

Meeting Traffic

9 Cars are pulling out from the road on the left. Prepare to allow them to enter the road you are in.

10 A removal lorry is creating a narrow gap for you to pass. Oncoming vehicles have priority over you. Make sure you position your car out to have a look along the road before passing the lorry.

11 Prepare to hold back and allow the red car through.

12 Remember here that if you are going to turn right you must give way to the lorry approaching in the opposite direction.

1 You must give good clearance with the car in front of you around parked vehicles. The driver in the car ahead might find a space to nudge into that could not accommodate you should a vehicle appear in the opposite direction.

2 You need to give good clearance around parked cars. The gap should be about a door's width from the parked cars, which is around three feet.

3 You must not stop on a pedestrian crossing. So be prepared to stop before the crossing and wait until you have at least a car's length beyond the crossing before driving forward.

4 Keep the junctions on the left side of the road clear. This will allow vehicles to enter. Think about the possibility of an emergency vehicle wanting to enter the road.

Adequate Clearance

5 You must maintain good clearance behind a vehicle in a general drive, but you should drive up to the speed of the traffic flow.

6 Look for road markings. Hold back if you do not have clearance beyond the 'Keep Clear' markings.

7 You must maintain good clearance around cyclists. Remember cyclists do not travel in a straight line.

8 A removal lorry is causing an obstruction. Hold back about two or three car lengths so that you can see around the lorry. Position your car towards the middle of the road and stay within your lane to avoid blocking the road. The road beyond the lorry looks congested with the bus turning. You can see a lorry approaching from the right, behind two cars.

1 Look along the pavement to your left and you can see a child approaching on a bicycle. Anticipate that the child could enter the road in front of you, reduce your speed and prepare to stop if necessary.

2 You can see people off-loading goods from a van. Anticipate that the item they are holding could drop in front of you. Maintain a speed where you could stop safely if necessary.

3 The car in front has a right indicator on. Anticipate that the car could pull out before you. There is the possibility the driver might want to take the entrance on the right or drive straight on.

4 A car is approaching the junction from a road on the left. Anticipate that the car could emerge into your road before you drive past the junction.

5 A post van is parked opposite you. Anticipate that the postman may return at any moment. The post van will make frequent stops so you need to be aware of the hazards caused by such a vehicle.

6 A red van is parked on the left. Anticipate that the driver's door could open before you pass it. Look for feet under the van to see if anyone is the other side of it.

7 The end of the school day is around three thirty in the afternoon. Anticipate that pupils could cross the road at any moment. Reduce your speed and prepare to make a stop if necessary and safely.

8 A rear door is open along the parked cars on the left. Anticipate that the person you can see could walk out from the parking area.

9 A car is reversing. Anticipate that the car could enter the road without the driver taking effective observation.

10 Approaching a green traffic light. Anticipate that the light could change at any time. Approach at a speed where you could stop safely if necessary. Never increase your speed when the light is green. Regard the green light as the most hazardous of all the light colours.

11 A removal van is reversing into your road. Anticipate that the van could move into your lane. Approach at a speed where you could stop safely if necessary.

12 Be aware of tradesmen round the lorry. They could be serving the shop on the left.

The Bus

1 A bus is parked on the left. If you see the bus with a right indicator on at about this point you should reduce your speed and allow the bus to emerge into your road. (Refer to the Highway Code)

2 You can see a bus lane on the left. You are not allowed to drive along this lane unless otherwise stated (where, for example, there are road works). You can turn into a driveway or into a road on the left. But you need to take good observation before attempting the manoeuvre.

3 Maintain a good clearance from the bus and anticipate that the bus might stop at any time.

4 This is a good distance to be away from the bus so that you can see to the right and along the road. If you are too close to the bus you will not be able to look out for oncoming traffic. Remember, if you can see the driver's mirrors the driver can see you.

5 Ahead is a lane only for cyclists and buses. The sign in the middle illustrates a bus and a bicycle. The sign could apply to a particular time of the day. For example, no cars should enter the lane ahead between 10 am and 4 pm.

6 The bus ahead has stopped. Anticipate that passengers could be disembarking from the bus but hidden from view.

The Dustcart

1 As you can see the wheelie bins are out. The wheelie bin on the immediate left appears to be full. This means you can expect to see the dustcart lorry in this area at any time.

2 Sometimes the dustcart may park awkwardly, blocking the road while rubbish is loaded.

3 The dustcart is parked on the right side of the road so you can expect to see workmen in the area.

1 The sign depicting children in this area. This sign could apply to a school, playground or a Patrol. Keep a good scan for young children as they have little understanding of road sense.

2 Elderly people are not able to move quickly. They could experience poor sight or hearing. Look out for them and give them time to cross the road. Have respect for them.

3 This is a sign informing you of a Patrol ahead. These children patrols are controlled by the "Lollipop" person dressed in yellow during the times children go to school or as school finishes. (See Pedestrian Crossings.)

4 The sign informs you of horse riders in this area. Prepare to reduce your speed if your observation down the road is restricted.

5 The sign you see here warns you to expect pedestrians on the road. Country roads do not have pavements.

6 This is a sign warning you of disabled persons. Keep your speed low and scan for them. Allow them plenty of time to cross the road.

7 This is a sign warning you that cyclists frequently use this road. Give good adequate clearance around them. Remember they have little protection on the roads.

8 This is a sign warning that children could be playing on the road. Note the new speed limit ahead.

9 Approaching a horse must be done at walking pace. Avoid any revving of the engine. Do not use the horn. Pass the horse with good clearance.

10 Ahead you see a sign informing you of a primary school on the left side of the road. Expect to see children around this area.

11 You are approaching a cyclist on the left. Hold back until you have room to overtake. Make sure you can see down the road ahead clearly and allow good clearance. Being too close could make the cyclist lose balance and fall off.

12 This is a good distance to be at this time from the horses. Notice the road corners to the left and dips downwards. There is nothing more you can do but hold back with good clearance until you can see well down the road.

13 The motorcyclist is a vulnerable road user. This is because motorbikes are fast vehicles and, due to their narrow appearance, they are hard to see clearly against larger vehicles. They can "hide" around a lorry for example. You need to take good observation at all junctions, especially after a large vehicle has passed you.

Emergency Vehicles

1 An ambulance is approaching with the blue lights on. The car on the right is pulling over. You should come to a stop at this point. That will allow enough space for the ambulance to pass.

2 An ambulance is on the right with the blue lights on. You should reduce your speed and anticipate that the ambulance will pull off at any time. You must prepare to give way to this vehicle.

3 These are lights to warn you of fire engines using the fire station on the left. The order of lights is as follows: First you will see the amber light beneath the two red lights come on. You should prepare to stop. Then the alternating red lights are activated.

4 When you hear the sound of an emergency vehicle check behind through your mirrors as well as ahead of you and to the sides. It is not always easy to know exactly where the sound is coming from. Once you have sighted the vehicle make sure it has room to pass. You can see the car in front of you has pulled right up against the kerb.

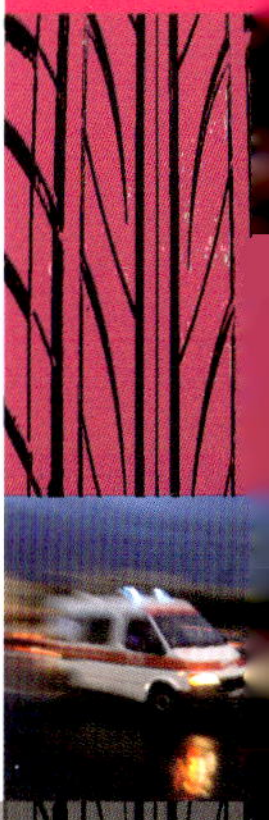

Cyclists

1 Hold back at the white line before the red cycle box.

2 The Cycle Lane is on the left side marked out by broken white lines. You must avoid driving along the Cycle Lane. Only cross the lane if you are turning into a drive or road. Make sure you carry out good observation before doing so.

3 A cycle race is approaching you from the opposite direction. Be aware of cyclists in the middle of the road coming round the corner. Pull over towards the kerb on your left and reduce your speed.

4 Allow the cyclists to exit the junction. Maintain good separation.

5 Keep a good separation from the cyclists, while driving in a restricted area. Remember when considering an overtake, to treat two cyclists in line close to one another like passing a medium-size car.

1 This sign shows a large complex junction that links a motorway (blue background) and a primary route (green background). In addition there is a secondary sign nearer to the point of entry showing primary routes only. It is very important to position your car in good time for the exit you want to take when leaving the junction. For any exit that is greater than the 12 o'clock position you need to be in the right lane on the approach. Look for arrows on the road surface. Some junctions may have three lanes at the point of entry. Depending on the arrows or road markings, it may be possible to be in either two of the three lanes at the point of entry. Typical road markings at a large intersection might be M25 (W), A22 (N) and M25 (E).

2 This is a mini roundabout. Taking the first exit you need to be in the left (nearside) lane.

3 As you can see by this sign roundabouts are not always 'round' in shape.

4 This is a medium size roundabout. Note that the first route connecting the roundabout is one way leading to the junction, so you cannot take this road. If you want to travel to Tonbridge Town Centre or Maidstone you should position your car to enter the right point of the entry bay, because the exit is greater than the 12 o'clock position. Follow close to the island on your right in a clockwise direction. As you pass the Southborough exit check your main (interior) and left mirrors, then indicate left and steer away into the new road.

5 You want to take the road to Crowborough. First you must check your main and right mirrors. Position your car towards the right side of your lane on the approach but do not drive over the white lines on your right. Then observe in good time to your right close to the island and to the point of entry from the road on the right. If it is clear then steer clockwise round the island. As you pass the first exit, look into your main and left mirrors, then indicate left and peel away from the roundabout into the new road.

6 You are approaching a mini roundabout. Reduce your speed in good time and take early effective observation. Look over the hedge to your right to check for oncoming vehicles approaching. You must give way to traffic coming from the road on your right as well as traffic turning around the roundabout island.

7 You are in the right lane to take the third exit. The lorry on the left has not indicated left so you must assume it is not taking the first exit. It is most likely going to take the second exit, which is in the 12 o'clock position.

8 You are going to take the second exit. This is marked by a straight arrow on the road. Some roundabouts have arrows marked out on the road to help you position yourself in good time. But arrows are often marked out where there is a requirement for traffic to be positioned differently from the normal expected lanes. This is possibly due to a high volume of traffic coming from a particular road. In this situation it is better to split the traffic flow up into two specific lanes to avoid congestion.

9 You have positioned the car to take the third exit. At this point (as seen in the picture) you should have checked your main and right mirrors before applying a right indicator. The car is positioned for the right point of entry bay.

10 Look to the right in good time. The car on the right has straight front wheels, so this should give you the clue that it is not going to pass you. It would be safe to enter the roundabout now.

11 Follow round the island keeping in the right lane.

12 As you go past the last exit before the one you want to take check your mirrors to go left and then apply the left indicator.

13 At this point you must peel away from the right lane and enter the new road. Note the new speed limit ahead.

14 The red car in front is going right (second exit). Notice that it is holding at the point of entry to give way to the car turning in the roundabout.

15 As you can see there are two vehicles approaching the roundabout on your right side. The red van is in the left (nearside) lane and will take the road you are in (that's his first exit). The car is approaching in the right (offside) lane. This car is going past you. You must hold back as it is close to the point of entry. You can assume the driver of the car wants to take the road to your left or conduct a 'U' turn. You are positioned to take the second exit, where the car is coming from.

16 It looks clear to your right, so there is no need to pause at the point of entry.

17

18

19

20

17 The BMW on your right is entering the roundabout. You must hold position. Also look behind the BMW you will see another car that looks as if it is going to pass you as well. The lorry on the other side is leaving the roundabout. No vehicle is going to shield the emerging cars.

18 The car entering the roundabout has a right indicator on, so hold position and give way to it. There is also another car following behind. Looking across the island you see no vehicle that will shield them from you. Anticipate that the vehicle following will enter the roundabout without stopping. The silver car which is slightly hidden by the black car is in the nearside lane and will enter your road.

19 The car to your right is being shielded by a van. You can see the van has straight front wheels, so it is going to enter your road. It is very important to catch the shield of the van **before** it passes the exit on your right in order for you to make a safe entry. As the van starts to pass the mid point of the exit on your right you will have to assume that the car will start to emerge. If you are not able to catch the shield early then you must hold back and allow the car to pass you.

20 Here there is another shield. The car within the roundabout precinct is leaving into your road because its front wheels are straight. At this point you could enter the roundabout safely.

21 This is a close-up view of a mini roundabout. Just visible is a car in the right (offside lane) position. That car is going to pass you and enter the road on your left or carry out a 'U' turn. So you must hold your position and allow the car to enter the roundabout.

22 The lorry in the road ahead is still some way off from the point of entry. Looking across the island you see nothing to affect you, which means you can enter safely.

23 Approaching the point of entry. Prepare to pause at the point of entry as you can see a car is in the offside position.

24 This is another view of a mini roundabout.

25 Breaking away into the new road. Once you have vacated the roundabout and have entered the new road make progress and keep up with the traffic flow.

26 You are in the offside lane. The roundabout ahead has three points of entry. The lane you are in would be suitable to take the third exit. At this point check your main and right mirrors and then indicate right. And start to reduce your speed all the way to the point of entry.

27 Roads with single lanes in each direction, with speed limits of 50 mph or national, have count down markers on the approach to a junction. Each of the markers is separated by a gap of 300 feet. Carry out the Mirror – Signal – Manoeuvre routine as you pass the three bar marker.

28 Remember when you pass the final count down marker you have 300 feet to the point of entry.

29 This is a busy intersection and has three points of entry. You could enter any of the three lanes to travel to the 12 o'clock exit (the second exit). There are straight arrows at each arrival point. What you have to take into consideration is that if you enter the roundabout complex from the right lane, you have to take the inner lane initially and must then cross into the middle lane as you peel off into the new 12 o'clock exit. You will need to cover all your blind spots to your left, then indicate left before conducting the manoeuvre. There is the problem of filtering into the left lane of the new road when the traffic is dense. There is the risk of blocking the exit point. Taking the left point of entry would be your preferred choice for taking the road ahead.

30 Looking along the lanes within the same roundabout as in P29. The black car is in the middle lane and the two other cars are in the inner lane. They are all going for the second exit. You can see the white car is peeling away from the island. The black car behind has a left indicator on. Notice the silver car on the left (first exit) is giving way to the three cars on the roundabout. The arrow is pointing to the second exit.

31 The lorry has a left indicator on, which means it is going to take the first exit. However, the driver of the lorry did not take the first exit but the second exit! It is very important to indicate correctly, but because the lorry is long it is entitled to take the outer lane. So expect that large vehicles may use an outer lane for making a right turn.

32 This is a busy scene at a major roundabout.

33 The red car is holding back to give way to the two cars approaching from the right. The first car has the left indicator on and so it is going to take second exit to the left of the red car.

34 This is a traffic light controlled roundabout (Parliament Square). Traffic lights are installed when there is a high traffic flow from all entry points.

35 This is another traffic light controlled roundabout (Trafalgar Square).

Dual Carriageways

1 This is an over view of a dual carriageway. There are two lanes on each side of the central reservation area. These roads are not for stopping in. They have a maximum national speed limit of 70 mph. Lorries and vehicles pulling trailers are restricted to 60 mph. If it is safe to do so you must try and keep as close to the speed limit as possible otherwise to the traffic flow. A slip road to exit the dual carriageway can be seen on the left.

2 Here you can see the traffic heading away on the left side or nearside lane. The blue van approaching is also in the nearside lane. This lane should be used all the time unless you are overtaking. The inner lane is called the offside lane.

3 A car is joining the dual carriageway from a slip road. It is important to build up speed to the traffic in the nearside lane.

4 You are on the slip road. You must not enter the hatch markings on the right. Slip roads are designed for vehicles to build up speed to the traffic using the nearside lane on the dual carriageway.

5

6

7

8

5 The use of mirrors is vital and should be checked about every 6 to 8 seconds. If you are planning to move into the offside lane, you will need to check your main and right mirrors and look briefly to your right to cover all the blind spots. Remember a vehicle just to your right side may not be in a mirror but a blind spot. Do not indicate if there is a vehicle in the right lane close behind you. This could make the driver slow down unnecessarily or even swerve to think you are going to pull out. Make sure you indicate right, when there is a good spacing between you and vehicles behind you in the offside lane.

6 Stay in the nearside lane if the speed of the traffic flow is close to or on the speed limit. If you multiply your speed by 1.5 it will give you how many feet per second you are travelling. At 70 miles per hour you are moving at a speed of 105 feet per second.

7 This is another view from the slip road. Here you are about to join the dual carriageway. Only enter the nearside lane when you are passing the broken lines on your right.

8 Carry out a main and right mirror check and a brief look over your right shoulder then apply a right indicator. Keep your speed building up progressively to the speed of the traffic flow in the nearside lane and then steer into this lane. Stay in the nearside lane for a short while before thinking about moving into the offside lane if you need to overtake.

9 Here you are in the offside lane. You have to be seen to be overtaking to stay in this lane. The lorry on the left will not be permitted to speed above 60 mph. If you can do 70 mph then remember your overtaking speed is just 10 mph. It looks as if you can stay in the offside lane for the moment until you have passed the lorry. Keep good mirror checks whilst in this lane to see how close vehicles are behind you.

10 Entering a tunnel ahead. Stay in your lane and select dip headlights about this point. Remember to switch the lights off after exiting the tunnel.

11 You are in the nearside lane. Allow the car ahead to enter the dual carriageway from the slip road. You could consider moving over to the offside lane if it is safe to do so. Changing lanes will let you maintain your speed with the traffic flow. If you are not able to change lanes then reduce your speed.

12 Allow these vehicles to enter the nearside lane. Vehicles must not stop on the slip road.

13 In dry conditions you should be at least two seconds away from the car in front. Start to count very slowly as the car ahead passes under the bridge. If it takes two seconds or more for you to arrive under the bridge then you should be able to slow down safely without being too close to that vehicle.

14 The sign ahead is informing you of an exit coming up. Notice the three bar count down marker. As you pass the three bar count down marker carry out your Mirror – Signal – Manoeuvre routine. Do not slow down too much whilst you are on the dual carriageway. The slip road is for you to reduce your speed.

15 Just like all roads you travel on expect that road works could be in operation. This could affect your driving. Here you can see temporary speed sign of 40 mph.

16 Ahead you can see a temporary lane change sign. This is due to road works ahead. You need to respond to this information in good time.

17

18

19

17 This is a sign showing two exits ahead. If you are going to take the second exit, make sure you carry out your main and left mirrors check then indicate left as you are passing the first exit. Do not signal before the first exit. The sign is telling you the first exit is one mile away. Now in terms of time that is just one minute away if you are driving at 60 mph. At 70 mph that would be about 40 seconds away.

18 Once you have left the dual carriageway start to reduce your speed and expect to see a lower speed sign very soon. There could be a 30 mph sign in place before you leave the slip road.

19 This is another view of a slip road. Notice this slip road has a very sharp bend to the left.

1 Here a motorway is continuing to the left with two lanes, while the two lanes on the far right will form part of another motorway. You must not cross the hatch markings on your right. These markings create the separation between the motorways. Note the signs over the bridge are in blue signifying you are driving along motorways. The left sign informs you that you are continuing along the M25 eastbound. The right sign informs traffic on the right that they are joining the M20 eastbound.

2 Good separation is vital at high speeds. The stopping distance increases with speed. You are in the middle lane, which is an overtaking lane for traffic on the left (nearside lane). Under no circumstances should you increase your speed to pass vehicles on your right. This would be a dangerous manoeuvre because there are blind spots which means that the driver in the right lane may not clearly see you when you are about to pass him.

3 Remember we talked about the Two Second Rule in the dual carriageway section. Use a reference like a bridge for the vehicle in front of you to pass under and count very slowly. If it takes at least two seconds by the time you pass under the bridge then you have good separation in dry conditions. This increases to four seconds when the road is wet and 10 seconds if the road is slippery due to ice. Here you are driving in the nearside lane because you are not overtaking.

4 You are in a slip road leaving one motorway to join another. The left arrow on the sign shows that the lane you are driving in will form the nearside lane of the next motorway around the corner.

5 This is another slip road joining a motorway. Keep your speed up. Check your main and right mirrors and look to your right to cover all the blind spots. At the broken lines gently steer into the nearside lane. Remember at high speed you should avoid excessive steering. Steering feels much "lighter" the faster you drive.

6 On the bridge ahead you will see a temporary speed sign of 50 mph. These signs are centrally controlled. A lower speed might have been put in place due to heavy traffic, a possible accident further along the road, reduced visibility or wet surface. The signs can be switched to inform you of a lane closure, telling you to move to another lane. You should scan for these signs on bridges or along the central reservation area.

7 You are in the middle lane. The car on the right has the left indicator on, so anticipate that it is going to move into your lane. Give the car good clearance to move over.

8 A motorway sign on the left informs you that there is an exit one mile away. The lane to your left separated by a continuous white line is the "hard shoulder". You must not enter this lane unless you have broken down or have had an accident. There are emergency phones, which are a quarter of a mile apart. Use your hazard lights if you stop in the hard shoulder. Stay in your car once you have alerted the emergency services.

9 The electronic sign on the left is centrally controlled. This sign is to inform you of an important situation that could affect your driving. For example, it could be telling you that there has been a serious accident on another motorway that joins the one you are on ahead.

10 A car is emerging from a slip road. You must allow the car to enter the nearside lane. You could consider moving into the middle lane at this point to maintain good clearance from the car or, if that is not possible you may have to reduce your speed.

11 It is important to look for signs on bridges because they could affect your planning for having to make a lane change or remain in your lane. You can see the nearside lane is for the Dartford Crossing, Stansted Airport and Bromley. The middle and offside lanes are for Maidstone, Channel Tunnel, Sevenoaks and Hastings.

1 In the summer the growth of hedges and leaves on the trees make it hard to spot signs. You need to scan the sides of the road. Here you can see a 30 mph speed sign almost totally hidden from view.

2 Be aware of even slower speed limit signs. These are usually found in built-up areas as part of more rigid traffic calming measures. You may see these speed limits around primary schools, hospitals, housing estates or even in a busy high street.

3 This is a close view of a mandatory 30mph speed sign. If you are approaching a lower speed sign you must be at the lower speed **before** you pass the sign.

4 This is a well-marked-out road showing three 30 mph speed signs each with a yellow background.

5 A road surface 20 mph speed sign.

6 The speed camera on the left is clearly marked in bright yellow. These cameras are installed where there have been around four fatalities in four years.

7 These are lines that you see on the road as you approach or pass a speed camera. There are cameras that pick up speed of vehicles passing in either direction.

8 This is a solar-powered speed warning sign. These signs are very accurate and will activate on an oncoming vehicle approximately 300 to 400 feet away should the speed be in excess of the limit. This sign was activated by the car in front.

9

9 Remember the last speed sign you passed? Multiply your speed by 1.5 and it will give you how many feet per second you are travelling. At 50 miles per hour you are moving at a speed of 75 feet per second.

1 During the cold winter months, when there has been snow around, make sure you give yourself plenty of time before setting off. Allow the engine to warm up while you clear all the windows. Turn on the heater and have the fan running to the setting that allows warm air to blow on to the windscreen at full strength. If you have electrically heated front and back windows switch them on until all ice has cleared. It is also a good idea to check the coolant container under the bonnet and see that you have water and antifreeze between the minimum and maximum levels.

2 You should decide whether your journey is necessary or not. It might be a good idea to walk along your road and decide whether it is safe to move away from your parking position. When the layer of snow is several inches thick the car wheels may not be able to grip. Chains for the wheels might be beneficial in this case.

3 Move away in a less powerful gear than first gear. Second gear may prevent the wheels from skidding. Use the accelerator lightly.

4 You should allow good clearance between your car and the vehicle in front of you. Use the foot brake with care, as the road could be icy. Give yourself more time to slow down. In this picture this would be a good place to stop. Remember the phrase: "See a red light – show a red light".

All-weather Driving

5 Make sure all windows are clear of ice before moving away.

6 This is a wintry scene. There are shaded areas along the road caused by hedges and trees close to the road. You could expect ice on the road. Use your foot brake lightly but progressively in good time before the bends.

7 Keep a good "eye" on what is going on behind you. If the roads are icy you need to be conscious of how close vehicles are to you. A good adequate clearance is very important.

8 When the snow is beginning to thaw there is a very high risk of black ice on the road. The ice could be quite hard to detect as it could be just beneath some surface water.

9 Ahead you can see a fog bank. Make sure at this point you switch on your headlights (dipped) or fog lights or both. Start to reduce your speed. Remember to approach at a speed where you could stop safely if necessary within the distance you see to be clear.

10 If the visibility in fog conditions deteriorates, then keep reducing your speed. In extreme conditions you should not follow the red lights of a vehicle in front of you because you will be too close to that vehicle.

11 This is an autumn scene. The leaves are falling from the trees. Here the road is also wet. This road surface will be slippery. The wheels of your car may not have full grip of the road and that could result in skidding if you brake too firmly.

12 Another autumn day with leaves on the road.

13 After a heavy rainfall you could expect to find flooding on the road. To your left there is a fast-flowing stream. This might be as a result of a river bursting its banks or blocked drains. Avoid driving along the flooded area as it could seriously affect your braking. A condition like this one could result in your wheels aquaplaning.

14 The road here is descending and you see the water from the left is moving across the road. You should slow down in good time. It might be difficult to tell just how deep the water is at this point. If you drive too fast through this water your wheels could lose grip with the road making your steering very hazardous. Notice the wheels of the car on your right throwing up a lot of spray from the road.

15 You could expect to find flooding on the road at low points where there is a river with its banks close to the same level as the road after a severe storm. You must enter this area only if it is safe to do so. Select first gear, keep the revs of the engine not too low or too high and enter the flood around 5 to 10 mph. Try not to stop the car while travelling through this flood. There is the risk of water entering the exhaust pipe, which could result in the engine stopping. Once you have cleared the water check your brakes. This can be done by pumping the foot pedal several times.

16 Heavy rain can reduce the visibility even if you have the windscreen wipers on high speed.

17 On fast roads large vehicles can displace large amounts of water spray from their wheels. Maintain good clearance as your visibility could be reduced as a result of spray from large vehicles.

18 The rays of the sun on a damp road can be extremely hazardous by almost totally blinding your view down the road. Use of good sun glasses as well as lowering the visor above the windscreen in front of you could help.

19 Throughout the year when the sky is clear of cloud you could experience a combination of bright and dark conditions. Along this road there are over-hanging trees that create shadows. The problem you would face here is the delay in your eye pupils adjusting from the bright conditions into the shade. The pupil of the eye will close partially to prevent damage to the eye when there is bright light, but in dark situations the pupil opens out. The change from one to the other may not be quick enough. In the circumstance, you may well have almost no view into the shaded areas, producing practically no forward vision. Note you can see a cyclist in the shadow on the left.

20 Travelling in and out of shadows is one of the most hazardous conditions in driving. It is rather like standing in front of a lot of cameras with flashing lights on you. It can be a very disorientating experience.

Night Driving

1 The road bends to the left. Check to see if there is any reflection of lights from approaching vehicles. It looks clear at this point.

2 In a well-lit area you must use dipped headlights. Do not drive on sidelights. If your lights are on full beam, they could reflect in the mirrors of the vehicle in front, severely affecting the driver's ability to see ahead as well as behind.

3 Your visibility at night may be limited so you will need to reduce your speed even with full beam. Here the road bends to the right. Pedestrians might be hard to see if they are wearing dark clothes. If you see a pedestrian approaching from the opposite direction make sure you dip your headlights in good time. As soon as you see the lights of an oncoming vehicle reflecting on the road or to the sides, dip your headlights.

4 Looking into your main mirror you can see there is a car behind. If the lights appear to be bright you could deflect the main mirror by the switch at its base.

5 Driving in fog or rain you will need to use dipped headlights to avoid glare. These conditions at night considerably restrict visibility ahead. Drive slowly and prepare to brake on seeing a bend. Look for signs warning you of bends and junctions.

6 It is raining and a car is approaching. The wet windscreen of your car makes a blurry image of the headlights of the oncoming vehicle. The headlights of approaching cars can make it hard to see clearly down your side of the road.

Use of Indicators

1 If you are going to take the second road on your left, when would you indicate?

2 You want to take the next road on your right, but there is a fuel garage before that road. When would you indicate?

3 You want to change lanes on a dual carriageway. Why is it wrong to indicate with a car close behind you travelling in the lane you want to enter?

4 Is it mandatory to indicate before entering a new road?

5 If you are going to take the second exit at a roundabout, when would you indicate before exiting the junction?

6 What indicator would you apply before leaving a roundabout, left or right?

7 You are travelling in very slow traffic and you apply a left indicator early to take a road to your left. Why could the indicator that you have applied be misleading?

8 In the case of (7) when might it be better to apply the left indicator?

9 If you are slowing down but realise you cannot indicate at that stage, what signal could tell a car behind that you are reducing your speed?

Use of Mirrors

1 How often in a general drive should you be looking behind in your mirrors?

2 If you are about to overtake a parked vehicle on your left, what two mirrors would you use and in what order?

3 After passing the obstruction what mirrors would you use to come back to your normal lane position?

4 What is a blind spot?

5 Why do you need to check your mirrors before you increase and decrease your speed?

6 The wing mirrors are convex, what does that mean?

7 When looking through your interior (main) mirror what image do you see, actual size or smaller size?

8 Why is it important that you check your mirrors as soon as you have entered a new road?

Junctions Major to Minor

1 What is the first action you need to take before anything else on the approach to turn off into a minor road?

2 What is the most effective way of slowing the car down?

3 What hazards are you looking for at the beginning of a junction turning from a major road into a minor road?

4 How can you "tell" other road users that you are going to turn into a junction?

5 Is it mandatory to indicate before turning off into a new road?

6 After entering a new road why is it important to check behind through your mirrors?

7 On the approach to a minor road on your right, what would you do if you saw a car approaching from the opposite direction along your road?

6 What is meant by corner cutting?

9 What are the dangers of corner cutting?

10 How would you avoid corner cutting?

11 What hazards could you find along a new road you have entered?

12 Why is it dangerous to depress the clutch fully down unnecessarily on the approach to a junction without the intention to change gear or brake?

13 You see a traffic light controlled junction ahead and you want to turn right from the major road into a minor road, but you notice a yellow box. Where would you position the car to stop to allow cars to pass you before safely turning right?

Junctions Minor to Major

1 How would you know that a junction ahead of you requires you to make a mandatory stop before entering the major road?

2 Why are some junctions made to make you stop rather than just to Give Way?

3 What is the order of observation into this type of junction and give your reasoning for this?

4 Name a vulnerable road vehicle that can travel fast?

5 Where would you find an unmarked junction? Would anyone have priority within this junction?

6 Why is it important to have your steering wheel straight at the junction for turning right?

7 Where would you position the car for turning right?

8 Where would you position the car for turning left?

9 What is a 'closed' junction?

10 How would you identify a Give Way Junction?

11 Is it mandatory to stop at a Give Way junction?

12 What does it mean by the phrase "peep and creep"?

Pedestrian Crossings

1 Why is 'speed' the most important aspect in dealing with a pedestrian crossing?

2 Is a zebra crossing controlled or uncontrolled?

3 How would you identify a zebra crossing?

4 How could you tell that the lights of a Pelican crossing are going to change from green to red?

5 What does the flashing amber light mean at a Pelican crossing?

6 Before you slow down to a crossing what should you do?

7 Why is it unacceptable to wave someone across at a crossing?

8 What do you know about the zigzag lines on the approach to a pedestrian crossing?

9 How would you regard a crossing with an island in the middle, as a single crossing or a double crossing?

10 What do you know about a staggered crossing?

11 What do you call a crossing which takes both cyclists and pedestrians?

12 Is a Puffin a controlled crossing?

13 Are you allowed to stop on a crossing?

14 What type of crossing might you find around a school patrol area?

14 How can a blind person know that he/she has arrived at a pedestrian crossing?

16 How would a blind person know when it is safe to cross at a controlled pelican crossing?

The Horn

1 What time of the day must you not sound the horn of your car?

2 What does the horn mean in the Highway Code?

3 On a country road, when might you apply the horn?

Crossroads

1 Where might you expect to find an unmarked crossroad?

2 How might you identify an unmarked crossroad?

3 Who has priority at an unmarked crossroad?

4 Why do some cross road junctions have compulsory stop signs?

5 How would you identify a Give Way crossroad?

6 What would be the most acceptable way of observing into a crossroad junction? Left-Right-Ahead-Left? Ahead-Left-Right-Ahead? Right-Left-Ahead-Right?

7 If you approach a crossroad from a minor road to take the road ahead and you arrive at the junction at the same time as a car with a right indicator on from the opposite minor road, what would you do?

8 Why are some crossroads traffic-light controlled?

9 What is a staggered crossroad?

10 What routine would you use to go right at a crossroad from a minor road?

11 What do you know about "nearside to nearside" when turning right?

12 How would you know if a crossroad is designed for "nearside to nearside"?

13 What hazard is there turning right "nearside to nearside"?

14 What do you know about turning right "offside to offside"?

15 What is the main hazard for turning right "offside to offside"?

Meeting Traffic

1 If there is an obstruction on your side of the road, who would have priority, you or an oncoming vehicle?

2 Where would you position your car on the approach to an obstruction on your side of the road?

3 What type of arrow sign would tell you that you do not have priority over oncoming vehicles?

4 If you see an obstruction on the right side of the road but not on your side what precautions would you need to consider on the approach?

5 If you want to take the next road to your right, what would you do if you see a car coming from the opposite direction?

6 If you are approaching parked cars on both sides of a road and you see a vehicle in this area approaching you, what would you do?

7 Two vehicles are approaching in opposite directions between parked cars. Who has priority?

8 If you are travelling in a restricted area of parked vehicles on both sides of the road and you see a car approaching from the opposite direction, what are you going to be looking for in order to allow the car to pass safely?

9 Describe a warning sign that shows both sides of the road are narrowing ahead?

10 On a narrow country road what type of vehicle might you expect to see?

11 Why is it not acceptable to "flash" your headlights?

12 What is meant by "defensive driving"?

Adequate Clearance

1 What do you know about the Two Second Rule?

2 What road conditions might you expect where the Two Second Rule has to be doubled?

3 If you are driving around parked cars on both sides of the road, why is it very important to keep good clearance from the vehicle you are following?

4 What clearance should you give when overtaking parked cars?

5 Why do you need to check what is going on behind your car regularly through your mirrors?

6 If you have to hold back behind an obstruction why do you need to give good clearance from it?

7 If you cannot get through a pedestrian crossing due to heavy traffic ahead what would you do?

8 If there is a road on your left, where would you stop if the traffic ahead has come to a stop?

9 When you have stopped behind a car describe the phrase "Tyres and Tarmac"?

10 State three valid reasons for having adequate clearance between you and the car in front while stationary.

11 Why is it very important to maintain good clearance when overtaking a cyclist?

12 You see a junction with a Yellow Box. What must you not do?

Anticipation

1 What do we mean by the word "anticipation" in a drive?

2 If you see a child playing with a ball along a pavement, then suddenly the ball is accidentally kicked between two parked vehicles and heads across the road, what would you expect to happen next?

3 A pedestrian on the pavement on your left side looks anxiously towards you. What might you expect he/she could do?

4 You see ahead a car reversing from a drive. What might you expect the driver to do?

5 Why is a cyclist particularly hazardous?

6 What hazards might you expect around parked cars?

7 Looking through your main mirror you see a car getting very close to you. What could you expect the driver of that vehicle to do?

8 You see a man running towards a zebra crossing. What might you anticipate he could do?

9 You see traffic lights ahead at a controlled junction with a green light showing. What might you anticipate could happen next at any time?

10 You see two persons off-loading a piece of furniture from a van. What might you anticipate could happen at any time?

11 You are travelling along a country road and ahead you see mud that must have come from tyres. What type of vehicle could you expect to be using this road?

12 Name two vulnerable road users you could expect to find along a country road?

13 You see a gate open into a field. What might you expect to see along the road?

14 You are travelling along a narrow road and you notice damaged surface at the side of the road. What type of vehicle could be using this road?

15 You see a "wait sign" lit up in the yellow box of a Pelican crossing ahead. What might you expect could happen at any time?

16 You are travelling through a housing estate and you notice wheelie bins out beside the road. What could you expect to see along the road?

17 Why is a post van a hazardous vehicle?

18 How could you tell if there is anyone on the far side of a parked vehicle?

19 You are travelling on a narrow road and you see on each side of the road a long white line. What do you think this means?

20 Why do think it is important to sound your horn before a sharp bend with high hedges on either side?

The Bus

1 You are approaching a bus from behind that has its right indicator on at a bus stop. What would you do?

2 What hazards would you expect to see around stationary a bus?

Vulnerable Road Users

1 Why are elderly persons vulnerable?

2 The very young are also vulnerable. State your reasons.

3 How would you approach a person on a horse?

4 Name a fast road user that is vulnerable and could appear at a moment's notice along a road.

5 Give your reasons why a cyclist needs to be categorised as vulnerable.

Roundabouts

1 Why do you think it is important to take early effective observation into a roundabout?

2 Do you always have to stop at a roundabout?

3 If the road you want to take is greater than the 12 o'clock position, where would you position yourself at the point of entry? In the nearside or offside position?

4 What two mirrors would you use before exiting the roundabout?

5 At what point would you carry out the mirror check in the case of (3) above?

6 How would you "tell" other road users that you are going to take the next exit?

7 If you are going to take the second exit (which is the road in the 12 o'clock position), which lane at the point of entry would you be in? Nearside or offside?

8 Would you indicate on the approach in the case of (7) above?

9 In the case of 7 above at what point would you carry out your mirror check and indicate left before exiting the roundabout?

10 Your instructor says to you: "I would like you to take the first exit off the roundabout ahead". What routine would you use on the approach?

11 How would you tell if a vehicle at the point of entry on your right is going to pass you?

12 You see a vehicle within the roundabout about to shield a vehicle at the point of entry on your right. When do you think it is safe to enter: (a) Just before it passes the point of entry on your right or (b) As the vehicle is passing the point of entry on your right?

13 How can you "tell" a vehicle is clinging to the island as it appears in your visual scan?

14 Some large vehicles may circumnavigate a roundabout in which lane?

15 Large busy roundabouts may have three points of entry all with straight arrows on the road surface. You want to take the road ahead in the 12 o'clock position. Which lane at the point of entry would you think is the best to take?

16 Why do you think it is very important to curve with the roundabout rather than to travel in a straight line?

17 Some roundabouts are traffic-light controlled. Why do you think this is implemented?

Dual Carriageways

1 What is the purpose of a slip road joining a dual carriageway?

2 Why is it very important to keep your speed up with the traffic flow?

3 What is the maximum speed for lorries and vehicles pulling trailers on dual carriageways?

4 What is the maximum speed for cars on these roads?

5 Is stopping allowed on a dual carriageway?

6 If you are not requiring to overtake a moving vehicle, which lane should you be driving in, nearside or offside lane?

7 Is it acceptable to travel at a greater speed than a vehicle on your right? If not why not?

8 You see ahead vehicles approaching the dual carriageway from a slip road on your left. What might you decide to do?

9 You see a sign on the left indicating your exit is 1 mile. If you are travelling at 60 mph, how long will it take to arrive at the slip road?

10 Using the Two Second Rule, what visual reference could help you start to count very slowly in respect of the car in front?

11 A large vehicle is in front of you travelling at 60 mph; you can see you are closing up to this vehicle at 70 mph. What would be your overtaking speed if your speed is maintained at 70 mph?

12 You are coming up to your exit to leave the dual carriageway. You can see there are three count-down markers. What approach routine would you carry out as you pass the first marker with three bars?

13 Once you have vacated the dual carriageway, you notice there are no speed signs at the next junction. What is the speed limit in the new road which has a single lane in each direction?

14 If you are travelling at 70mph how many feet per second are you travelling?

Motorways

1 What colour signs would you expect to see along motorways?

2 If you hold a provisional licence are you entitled to drive on motorways?

3 What sign information could you expect to see over bridges of motorways, when there is poor weather ahead or traffic congestion?

4 If you see a sign lit up on an overhead bridge indicating your lane is about to close, what will you do in good time?

5 If your car is experiencing a problem and you are some way from an exit road, what would your course of action be?

6 You see a car ahead with its hazard lights on. What do you think the driver of the car is relaying to you?

7 If you have no mobile phone with you to contact an emergency service, what other facility might there be along the hard shoulder?

8 If you are travelling a long way on motorways, about how long should you drive for before thinking about going into a service area for a short break?

9 You want to change into a lane to the right along a motorway. What routine would you use to achieve this manoeuvre safely?

10 Before setting off on a long journey, what preparations would you expect to do concerning the drive?

11 Once you have vacated a motorway and have joined a slip road to take you on to a primary road, what mandatory signs should you look for?

All-weather Driving

1 What would you expect to see along roads in the autumn?

2 How could the effects of what you see on the roads in (1) above affect your braking?

3 If you use excessive speed through a flooded part of the road, what could happen to your wheels?

4 If you entered a sharp bend on a wet road and the car skidded to the right, what action should you do to correct the car?

5 Where is the front of the car facing in a right skid?

6 If you see a flood across the road ahead, what should you consider before entering it or turning around, bearing in mind the level of water in relation to your vehicle?

7 If you decide your car can enter the water how would you control the drive through it?

8 What do you need to check once you have gone through the flood?

9 What are fog banks?

10 If you see a fog bank ahead what do you need to do before you arrive there?

11 If you are driving in poor visibility and you see a car's rear lights on ahead of you, what clearance do you think you have between you and that vehicle? Good? Too close?

12 What are the dangers of driving along a road when the snow is beginning to thaw? State your reasons.

13 What preparations do you need to make if you are about to drive, but you see the car covered in snow?

14 What equipment might you use on your wheels if the roads look icy?

15 In order to avoid the wheels from skidding as you set off, what might be a suitable gear to use in snow conditions?

16 In very cold conditions, what do you need to check within the engine area to see you have a good supply of to prevent your radiator from freezing up?

17 What reservoirs in the engine require checking in the case of icing?

18 What are the hazards of low sun and shadows?

19 How does the sun and shadows affect your eyes? Explain what happens to the eyes when it is very bright.

20 What debris could you anticipate seeing along a country road after high winds?

Night Driving

1 You are travelling along a dark country road and there is a sharp bend ahead with high hedges on either side. How could you tell that a vehicle is approaching the bend from the opposite direction?

2 If you see dazzling lights in your main mirror what could you do to reduce the glare?

3 You notice a reflection of lights ahead along a hedge. What should you do to your headlights to avoid blinding the driver of the approaching vehicle before the car comes into view?

4 There is a car approaching you in heavy rain. What are the hazards you could expect to be confronted with?

5 Why are pedestrians particularly hazardous along a narrow country road at night?

6 A car overtakes you. What should you do to your headlights?

7 You are travelling in a well lit up area. What lights should you use?

a Side lights

b Headlights on full beam

c Dipped headlights

Write briefly what hazards do you see in the three pictures below and state what action you might need to take.

PROFILE

In January 2000, after a career in the insurance industry, I switched to driver education, qualifying as an Approved Driving Instructor and registering with the Driving Standards Agency. I franchised myself with the Central Instructors' Association Driving School. Now I am working for myself. I enjoy my new work and find the high quality of teaching required challenging and very rewarding.

In 2001 I qualified as a mentor with Rainer Kent Mentoring and, supported by Kent County Council, help young people coming out of care homes. For this voluntary work role I have attended a number of additional training courses on drug abuse, mental health and work involvement of Connections (a government organisation) for helping young people into work training experience and jobs. I am working to qualify for the B-Tech Award qualification.

A member of the Royal Ashdown Forest Golf Club, I enjoy playing golf, tennis, walking and swimming. I hold both British and Canadian Private Pilot's Licences and enjoy classical and jazz music.

Andy Hall

Institute of advanced Motorists

Driver Improvement Trainer Qualification

RPS Rainer Certificate in Mentoring

DIAmond Special Test

The Register of Approved Driving Instructors (Car) Hazard Perception Assessment